THERE IS A WAY

*The artwork reproductions
in this volume
are from original works by
Nancy Russell Nadzo*

THERE IS A WAY

MEDITATIONS FOR A SEEKER

Stefan C. Nadzo

*Artwork By
Nancy Nadzo*

EDEN'S WORK
Publisher

Copyright © 1980 by Stefan C. Nadzo and Nancy Russell Nadzo

All Rights Reserved

Library of Congress Catalog Card Number: 80-66831
ISBN: 0-937226-00-9

Printed by Coleman Graphics, Inc.
Farmingdale, Long Island, New York

First Printing .... June 1980
Second Printing .... February 1981

EDEN'S WORK

Happy are they who seek Truth with their whole heart.

Psalm 119

TABLE OF CONTENTS

AUTHOR'S NOTE	1
GETTING TO THE WAY	5
THE SOLUTION IS SPIRITUAL	10
THE EGO	33
THERE ARE NO EXPERTS	51
THE WAY IS TO SIMPLIFY	69
AND WHAT OF GOD?	91
LET US PRAY	103
STARTING ON THE WAY	117

AUTHOR'S NOTE

The spiritual search is the most important journey any of us will ever undertake. It is the only one that matters. It is all that matters. Early on in the journey it becomes clear, dimly at first, but increasingly over time, that there is nothing -- no thing, however defined -- that is purposeful or relevant to life but the interminable, unavoidable reach for Truth. It is that realization and the process that flows from it that is meant by the *way*, and the way is what this book is about.

Everything written here is personal; which is to say, each thought has come of my own inner struggle to See, and has been presented as I see it now. That some part of these contents might have meaning for or give direction and encouragement to other seekers is my hope and the reason for their publication. That this might not be the case is, I recognize, quite possible; for the journey to spiritual realization is by its nature a personal one, and while the landscape for all of us is similar, each will see it and describe it in the light of his current condition, and in that we are all different.

I said that the material here has been

offered as I see it now, and I stress the word *now*. With every step of this search vision changes, with each stage of growth our understanding of what has gone before is altered. Thus, we can speak only from where we are today, and today I see it as presented here. I am fully aware that there lies much difficult terrain ahead, and that for the treading of it I will change and so too will my view of these thoughts. The only guarantee against eventual revision is the alternative not to speak at all, and it is a valid one, chosen by many. I have opted for the other because it seemed right at the time of choice; that too may be seen differently ahead.

    A brief word about the format of this book may be helpful. The reader will notice that it consists of a series of individual thoughts interrupted by some of the same ideas treated at greater length. Each entry has been the subject of my own meditation along the way and was born of it. Those that have been expanded upon are ones which were particularly difficult for me to accomodate and which therefore seemed to warrant additional discussion. These essays, if that's what they are, are not intended to exhaust their subject, not in any sense to cover its every aspect and ramification, but merely to assist the reader in his own exploration of it.

On a matter of procedure, the reader will see that I have used capitals for the first letter of certain words. My purpose there is simply to indicate ideas or concepts which are intended to convey a meaning greater than or different from that which the words employed carry in normal usage. So that, for example, I may write God with a capital *G* because while I don't know exactly what I do mean, I think I know what I don't mean, and god, with the lower case, seems to me more the latter. Were there a better word, I would have used it. I expect that in the final analysis, there is no word. But we aren't there, and we start from where we are, with the tools -- in this case, language -- at hand.

Finally, there is nothing in this book that you don't already know. And more. If you would but see it.

GETTING TO THE WAY

There is a way, and you can find it. Many others have, and so can you.

But there is no point in looking around you for it, not among your friends and things. For those who have found it tell us that the way is not of this world. It is, they say, something altogether other, different from everything else we know -- beyond the senses we rely on for knowledge. But we can know it, as others have; on this point their experience is clear.

If the way is *not* of this world, how do we who *are* seek it? By wanting it, they say. Not like wanting a bigger house or a better paying job; more like the thirst for water after a desert drought. Or for the warmth of the sun after a winter's darkness. Like that, only more so. Perhaps when the pressures of this life and the dissatisfaction with its rewards grow sufficiently intense, when we want a way out of it more than we want any of the things we can accumulate by it, perhaps then we seek in earnest. Perhaps then we want the way.

And where do we look for this way that is nowhere around us? Precisely where we are, and as we are. For there is simply nowhere else we can begin to look; we can start only from wherever we are right now.

There is a way. That in itself is good news. But, even more, we are told, there is a way suited to each of us, personally tailored to meet the needs and capabilities of the kinds of people we are at this moment. So the way is many. And you will know your way, the teachings assure us, when you have found it. Like meeting an old friend or hearing a tune from the distant past; it feels good all over, and you know it instantly. Again, it's not that, but something like that.

One way to find the way to the way, if not the way itself, rests in the proposition that in order to find something which is beyond our senses, by which is meant to include our every faculty for perception, we have somehow to stop the activity of the senses, to transcend them. Seek senselessness. One way to do that seems to be to occupy the mind -- the senses' director and distribution center -- in pursuing a self-defeating proposition: a question or problem that is by definition beyond the capacity of the mind to resolve. Like describing the boundaries of infinity. Or the face of God. Or imagining the sound of one hand clapping. This is an undertaking which has to be adopted quite conscientiously; the mind must not realize your intentions, or it won't play along.

This volume is composed of thoughts generated by that process, and distilled from a vademecum, a form of personal journal developed over years along the way. They do not necessarily mean anything, and there is nothing particularly special about any of them. Many will appear childlike oversimplification, others even sheer nonsense. They may all be that. But with a little effort and some luck, you might manage to get one so stuck in your brain that it rattles around like a pebble you can't quite shake loose. And that process, the rattling and shaking, may frustrate and tire the mind enough that for just a quarter of a fraction of a microinstant, it will break stride, and then ... silence. Resounding, empty yet pregnant silence. And you are on your way.

Of course, just as soon as you notice it, it's gone again, obscured by the act of noticing, the mind in step again, and the accompanying noise. But you try again.

So, now you're on your way. Whatever happens, do not confuse this book with the way itself. At the very most, what this book -- or any book -- can be for you is a guide, a signpost indicating where others have gone and where you too can travel, if you wish. It should also provide encouragement; reassurance that there is a way and that you can find it. It might even serve as a tool to help pry open the closed doors, brush aside some of the veils. And it can be a friend: the companionship of another who, like you and with you, is seeking the way. But the way is yours, and only you can find it, with or without this book.

There is a way. Seek it. You *will* find it.

Whatever the problem, the solution is spiritual.

Whatever the suffering, the relief is spiritual.

Whatever your question, the answer is within.

That's the way.

THE SOLUTION IS SPIRITUAL

Whatever the problem, the solution is spiritual. This one thought says it all; it is the beginning and the end. Everything else along the way depends upon and flows from this assertion. Until you have undertaken to come to terms with this concept, you will not have begun; when you do, the rest can follow.

Whatever the problem, the solution is spiritual. *Whatever* the problem. Notice that the statement is all inclusive, allowing for no exceptions. And it means precisely what it says: whatever difficulties or discomforts you encounter in life, however minimal or gargantuan they may appear, their resolution rests in recognizing your spiritual-ness. This is the single most important consciousness altering concept you will wrestle with, for it stands against, and ultimately denies, everything else you have been taught. And for that reason the temptation to reject it or at least to apply it only selectively, leaving most aspects of life's apparent difficulties to traditional problem-solving methods, will be almost constantly felt and deceptively convincing. But keep working at it, for it promises nothing less than total liberation from fear, frustration, stagnation, anger, insecurity, and doubt. From those to complete and unremitting joy. And if those are the stakes, and they are, then who could want to choose differently?

The root of the matter is that we consider our problems to be external events, caused externally and occurring externally. Beyond that, we think of ourselves as external events too: physical things (bodies) in a world of myriad other physical things. So long as we see that way, we will seek to manage our lives (and resolve our problems) by manipulating external phenomena. Like chessmen on a board; each move is prompted by previous moves and determines future ones. Physical things bouncing back and forth off one another. And so each perceived problem creates reactions that in turn produce changed conditions from which new problems evolve. And so on. The trick is not to learn to play the game better, but to recognize that it is a game and to get out of it. To recognize that we are not physical things subject to other physical things in a physical world, but rather spiritual beings (in a *seemingly* physical world) whose nature is altogether other than what we perceive.

What we perceive. There's the difficulty. We have got to change our understanding of the perception process before we can proceed further. Consider this: despite what we may think, we do not see with our eyes, but with our minds. To be sure, it is the eyes that register light waves, but it is the mind, using the brain as a light wave deciphering tool, that determines for us what the information described by the light waves will mean to us, whether we will welcome what lies before us or be horrified by it. The eyes and the brain are simply devices which have no understanding of the data which they process. That's the function of the mind. In the same way, our problems are not external events, but impressions (opinions and judgments) of external events. Whether or not a thing affects us (and how it does so) is determined by what we consider to be our nature, and that is determined by the condition of our minds.

It is all in the mind, then, and that is where we have got to work first. Our understanding of life, our interpretation of events, our emotions and our reactions, all are determined by the direction and focus of our mental processes, our mindset. However we view life, so will we experience it. So, to change our lives, we have to change our minds. About ourselves. We have to discard our learned values which assume that ours is a physical world and that we are just objects within it, and adopt instead the conviction that our true nature is spiritual and then seek to see everything in the light of that conviction.

It's a process, not an instantaneous transformation. A little like constructing a building; you have to have the finished product in mind all the time, and every move you make, every decision you take, must be measured by the final goal. And your goal on the way *is* a new construction, a new you, and the way to get from here to there is by asking of your every thought whether it is born of and intended to assist the realization of that goal. At first, this will seem burdensome, impractical, and unproductive, for the tendency to revert to customary ways of thinking will be almost automatic and even apparently justified. We are all victims of inertia and creatures of habit. But the more often you remind yourself of your goal and insist on thinking in its terms, the easier will become the effort and the greater its rewards.

Your old self, governed by your old ways of looking at things, will attempt to assert itself almost constantly, too often successfully. And the more alert to it you become, the more will it try to deceive you into believing that it is not the old but the new. You can tell the difference though by restating your goal and again asking yourself if whatever is going on in your mind is predicated on the false premise that you are a physcial being in a physical world or is instead directed toward accomplishing your new purpose, reaching spiritual awareness by treading the way.

Whatever the problem, the solution is spiritual. Said longer, that might be put: your perceived problems depend for their meaning to you on your belief that you are of their world and therefore subject to them; deny that, asserting instead your spirituality, and everything will look different, no longer threatening, suddenly unifying -- *everything*, including what used to be perceived as problems.

Only the way solves problems without creating new ones.

Answers questions without raising new doubts.

The way is a way out and a way in.

Out of illusion and into Reality. Out of the ego, and into Spirit. Out of life, into Life.

The way is a lighted path.

But *you* must let in the light.

The way is knowing you can't look at a thing and at its reflection at the same time. Your focus is either on one or on the other. High or low.

The way, or not the way.

Look in the mirror.

What's there is not you, but an image projected by the ego. Like a movie.

Know that, apply it to your whole life, and things will begin to look different. Very different.

Better.

The way is a path to corrected vision.

The way is Seeing.

Seeing is no-thought; the absence of thought.

No-thought can be achieved through thought.

Think about it.

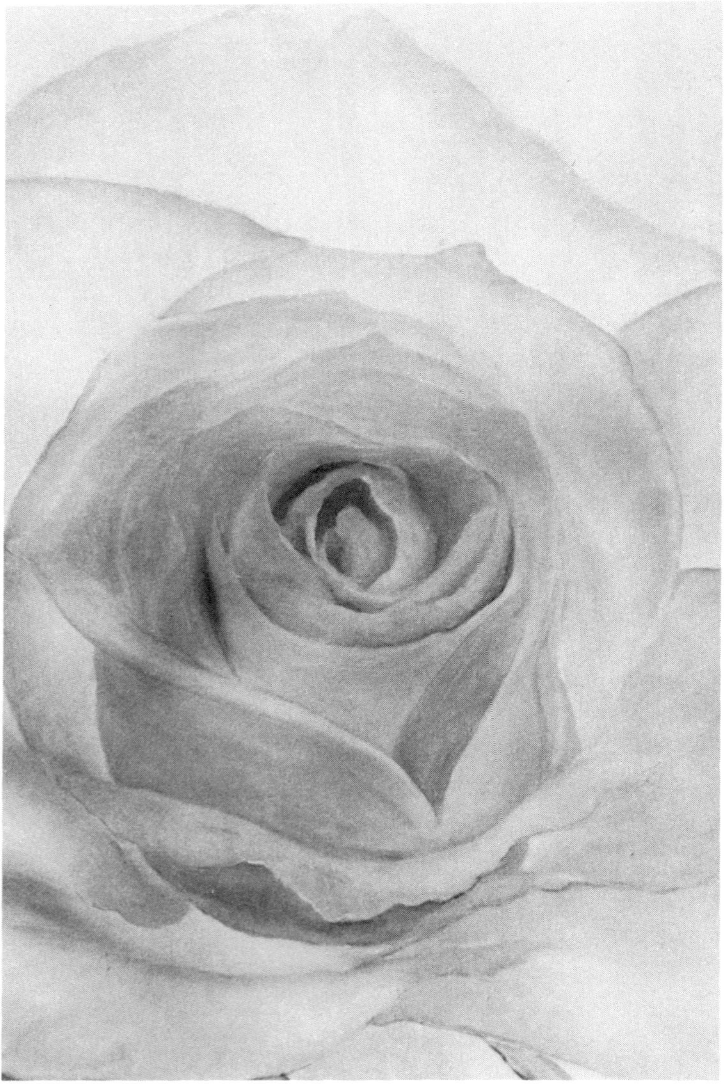

Thought is noise and preoccupies. In this, it is an enemy.

Thought leads to the way. In this, it is an ally.

Along the way, thought must cease, letting in light. Silence.

How will you know when you're on the way?

When the more you know the less you know.

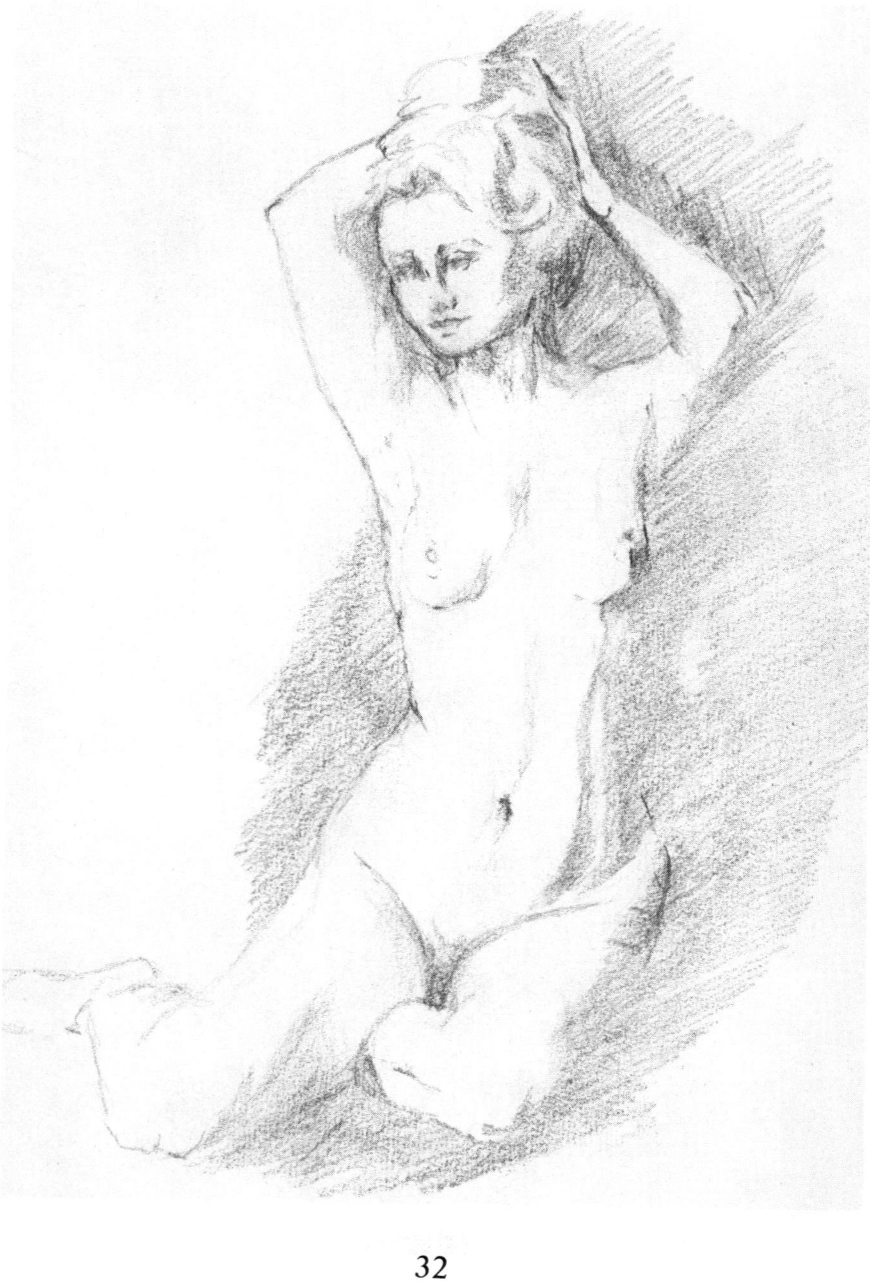

THE EGO

Ego sum. It's Latin, and translates "I am". And that, in two words, is the problem; the fact is, we aren't.

This word ego has numerous meanings in as many schools of psychology. For our purposes, the ego can be quite simply described as that aspect of ourselves which has convinced us that we are *selves*, separate entities, unique and distinct from other selves, entities, and things. Indeed, it is the ego that tells us there *are* others. The ego, then, can be understood as self-consciousness, consciousness of self. That's it. A few sentences, an easily grasped concept. And here the nightmare begins, because the truth is, we aren't selves. There is no separation. There are no things. All that is error, a grand illusion of the ego. What there is, is One; nothing more, nothing less. And that is what we strive to see by following the way.

But we are caught in a double bind: in order to see past the illusions of ego to Reality, we must transcend or silence the ego, blindfold its eyes, but as ego (and our identification with the ego is now virtually total) we cannot do so. The ego is itself part of the illusion and depends on it for existence;

how can it see what (from its view) is not? The ego cannot think past itself, and it is the ego which thinks.

Consider the schizophrenic as a possible parallel. (And by schizophrenia is meant here the condition commonly known as split-personality.) If a person absolutely believes he is Napoleon, so long as he is convinced of it, he cannot rid himself of the delusion, because his reality is not that he is a person who *thinks* he is Napoleon but that he is a person who *is* Napoleon. Accordingly, his response to suggestions for cure will be heard by Napoleon's ears, reacted to in Napoleon's terms, seen through Napoleon's eyes. His actual identity, the person he really is, will have been so deeply buried, so thoroughly factored out, as to be effectively unreachable. But for a cure to work, the identity beneath the delusion must be reached, the mistaken identity Napoleon circumvented.

However ludicrous the foregoing may be medically, it can serve as a learning device for us on the way. We are in a tragically real sense like a schizophrenic. On the one hand, we are not separate selves, but One Self (the schizophrenic's true identity). On the other, we think we are distinct entities (Napoleon), and our world of separate things seems real. And, again like the schizophrenic, our only hope for cure, for corrected vision, is, in the first instance, to recognize the error, and, in the second, to reaffirm as often and as earnestly as possible that recognition, so that it will increase in magnitude, and thereby strengthen the voice of our true Identity, however weak it may sound to us now, until it erases and replaces the error, ego, with Truth. And we -- the entity defined and created by the ego -- cease to exist, replaced by what it is that Is and always was.

For there *is* something (not a thing, but something). Somehow, even though as egos we cannot perceive it, we do sense that what we seem is not what we are, that there is more, something other. And, like our schizophrenic's true identity, this other has never ceased being despite our inability or refusal to see it. It is Eternal; it is All and One. And it, and only it, can say, as it does, I AM.

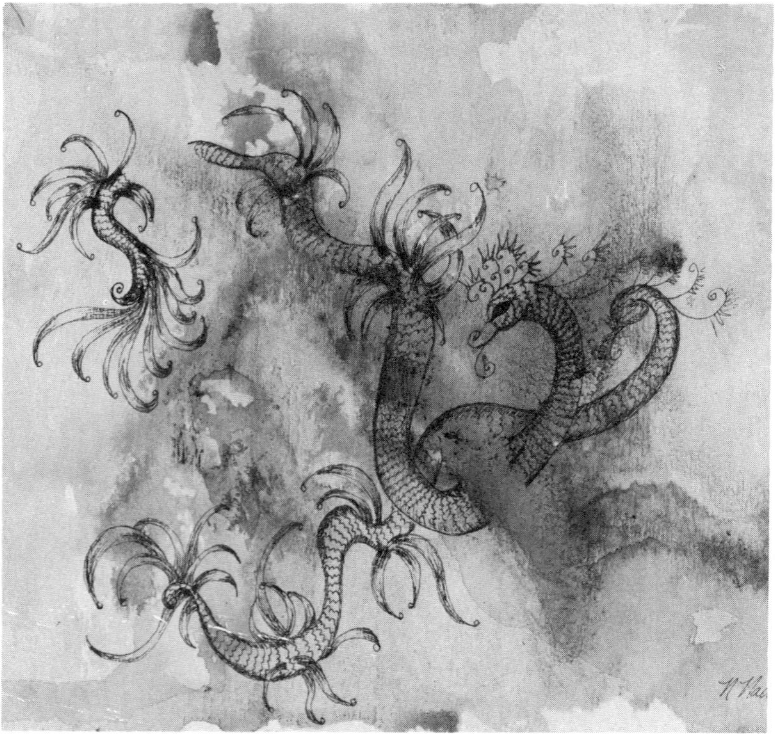

If there is an enemy, it is the ego. If there is a devil, it is the ego.

Every obstacle is created by the ego, for the ego. *Every* obstacle.

The ego can be overcome, and in so doing are you made free. That's the way.

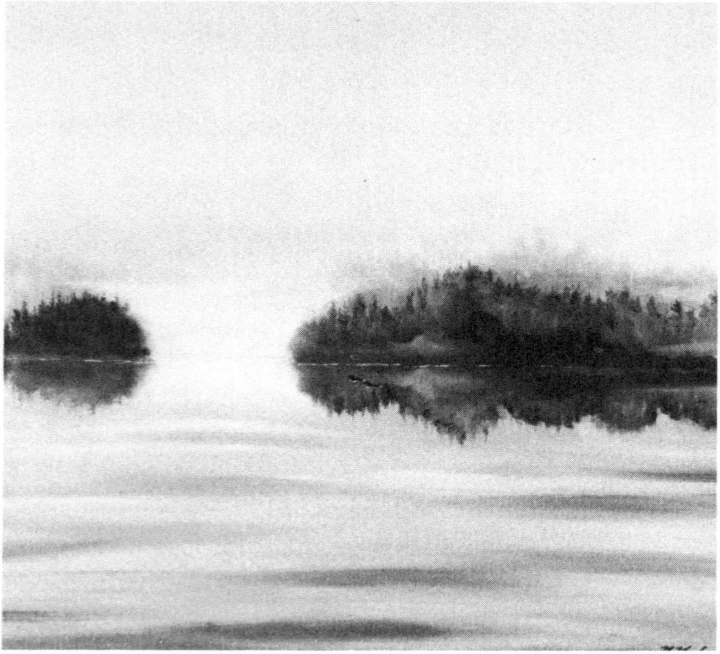

The way seems a lonely path, for loneliness is of the ego, and the ego doesn't want to go.

The ego is not an inherent part of you. It is acquired.

The ego is not a thing, but a point of view.

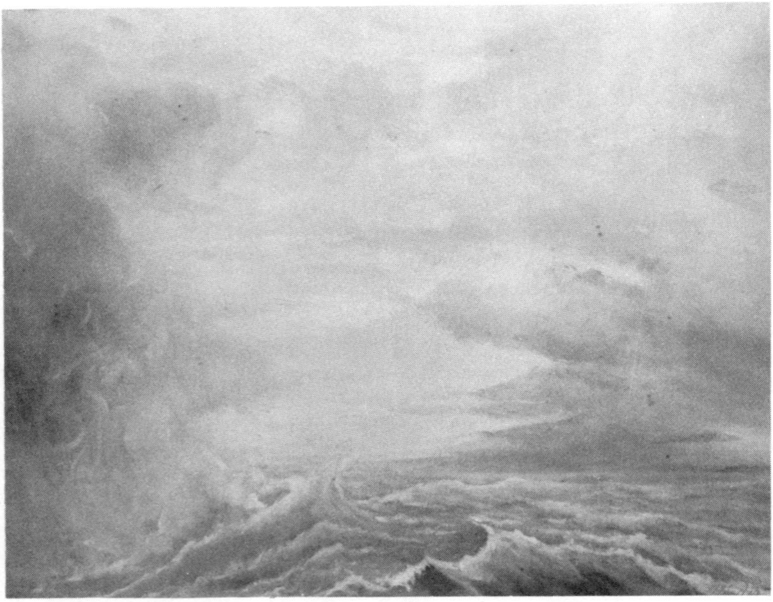

The ego is not what you think of yourself. The ego is *that* you think of yourself.

That you believe there is a yourself separate and distinct from other selves. That is the ego.

The ego is a misconception. Erroneous perception. The world seen wrong.

As an error, the ego can be corrected. Erased.

That is the way.

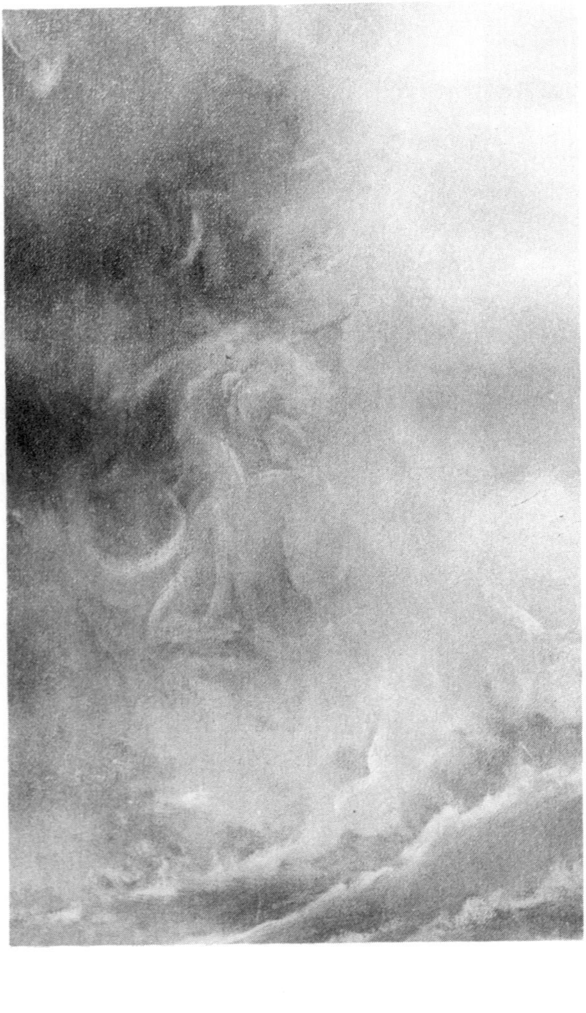

What is Real, your ego eyes cannot see.

What they perceive is illusion. Shadow viewed through a darkened lens ground by the blind.

But you start from where you are, with the tools at hand, seeking to perfect them, eventually to discard them. Along the way.

Time and space are meaningless illusions created by the ego to enclose and measure its things. Any meaning they hold for you has been granted by you.

And can be withdrawn.

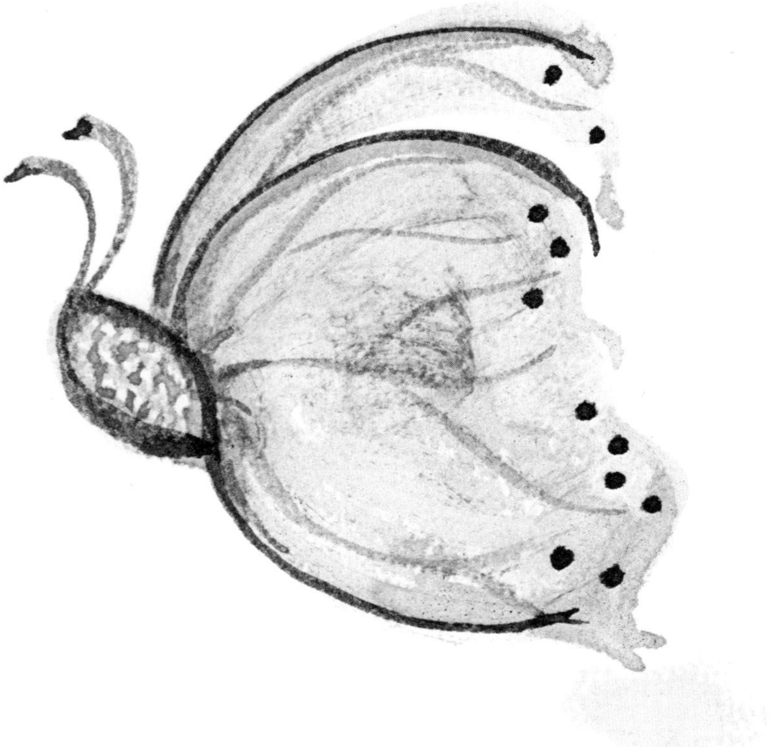

If time and space have any valid function, it is to serve as a medium in which to grow out of.

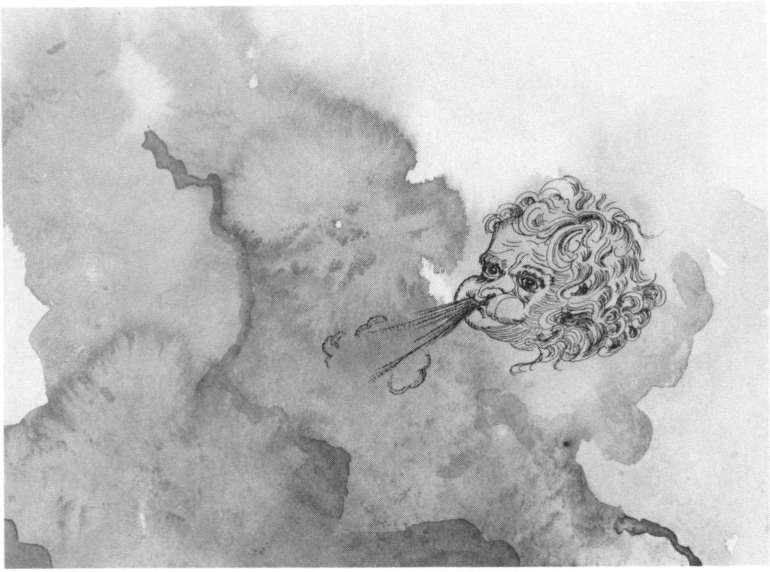

THERE ARE NO EXPERTS

If the way is a journey not entirely unlike another from place to place, are there not experts to whom one can turn, experienced travel facilitators, if you will, cosmic counterparts of travel agents, baggage handlers, express companies, and the like? It would seem there ought to be. And yet, even on an ordinary journey between two points on the globe, one wonders just how useful the experts really are. Is it not possible, even likely, that a travel agent, for example, might book you on a particular airline instead of another for reasons altogether unrelated to your needs (maybe he gets a kickback from them, or his brother flies for them) -- or he might send you through an intermediate stop or choose a flight schedule only because that is the course he has always adopted, and never considered any alternative routing. Finally, being human after all, might he not make a more serious error, possibly causing you to interrupt your progress? To be sure, you will likely get to wherever it is you are headed, but perhaps not in the least expensive or most expeditious way.

There are many already started on this journey you have just now undertaken. Like you, but ahead of you. They can serve as guides, and you would be foolish not to seek their advice. Having been there themselves, they are in a position to sense when you are in earnest or just playing, when you are moving too fast or getting in over your head; they can help if you have become bogged down or unnecessarily detoured. These guides and teachers can be found, and you will find them when you need them. Either in person or through books, lectures, among their students. And they will help if your call is genuine. But just as the ticket agent cannot complete your earthly trip for you, neither can your guides along the way. You must make the journey by yourself, one step at a time, and you can.

And in that sense, there are no experts. Only others who have gone before. Because however knowledgeable they may be, they cannot transfer their knowledge, and only you can know if their experience is relevant to your case. And only you can choose from among their teachings those aspects which are best suited to you as you are now. You must understand each step of the way as you take it, because unless you take it by considered choice it will not move you forward.

Finally, then, it should be clear that your best guide is within. Each of us has a Teacher that speaks to us in silence, that resides in that secret place so many other travellers have spoken of, and that, if we learn to listen in sincere surrender to His Infinite Knowledge, will not -- cannot -- fail us. *There* is our Expert, our personal and Universal Guide. More, there is the Way.

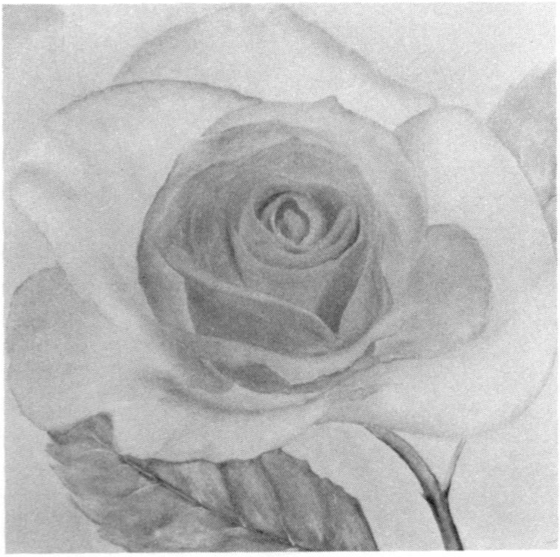

There are no experts.

Friends and guides, yes. Also, footprints left by others just ahead. Or a travelling companion beside you.

But each makes the journey for himself, in his own way, alone.

You in yours, me in mine. So, don't be pushed. And don't push.

Be open to impulse.

You have an inner voice. Listen to it. Trust it.

It rarely speaks in crowds. Often in silence.

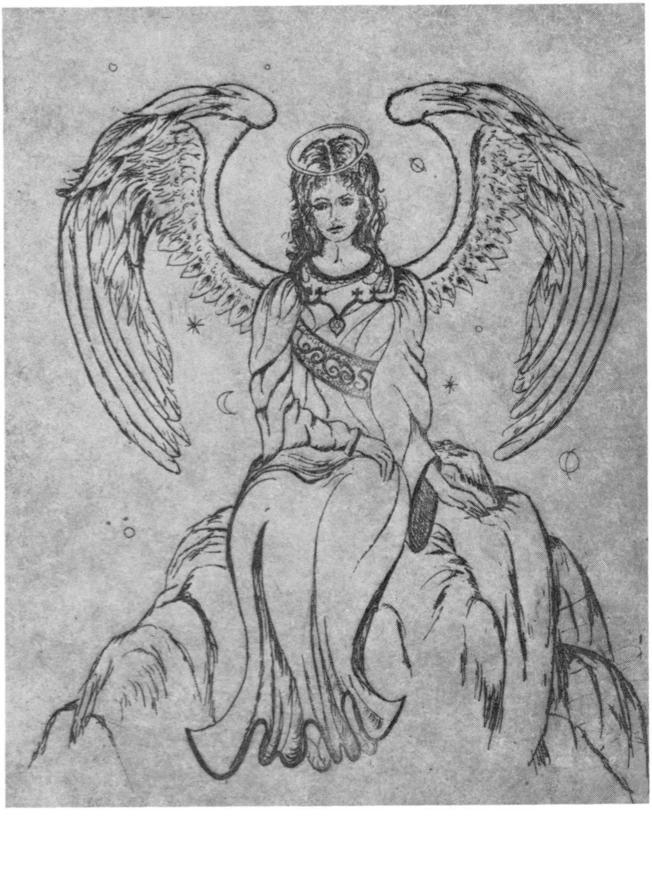

Take a spiritual master as an example. Any spiritual master. Use him as you would a map or a yardstick.

Not as an idol or the answer or a god. But as a guide or a pathfinder.

He too found the way and walked it.

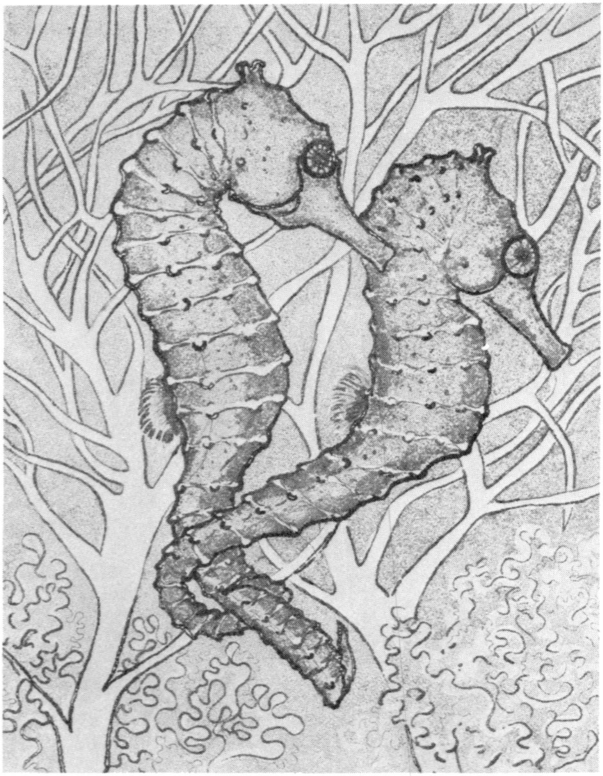

There is nothing special about any spiritual master that is not also special about you.

You are both equally ordinary.

Except he has found the way, and you are still seeking. He sees you as you are, and you see him as he isn't.

The difference between you, then, is simply optics.

What any spiritual master has accomplished, you can accomplish. Eventually, you must.

That is the way, and the way is inevitable.

Not if, but when.

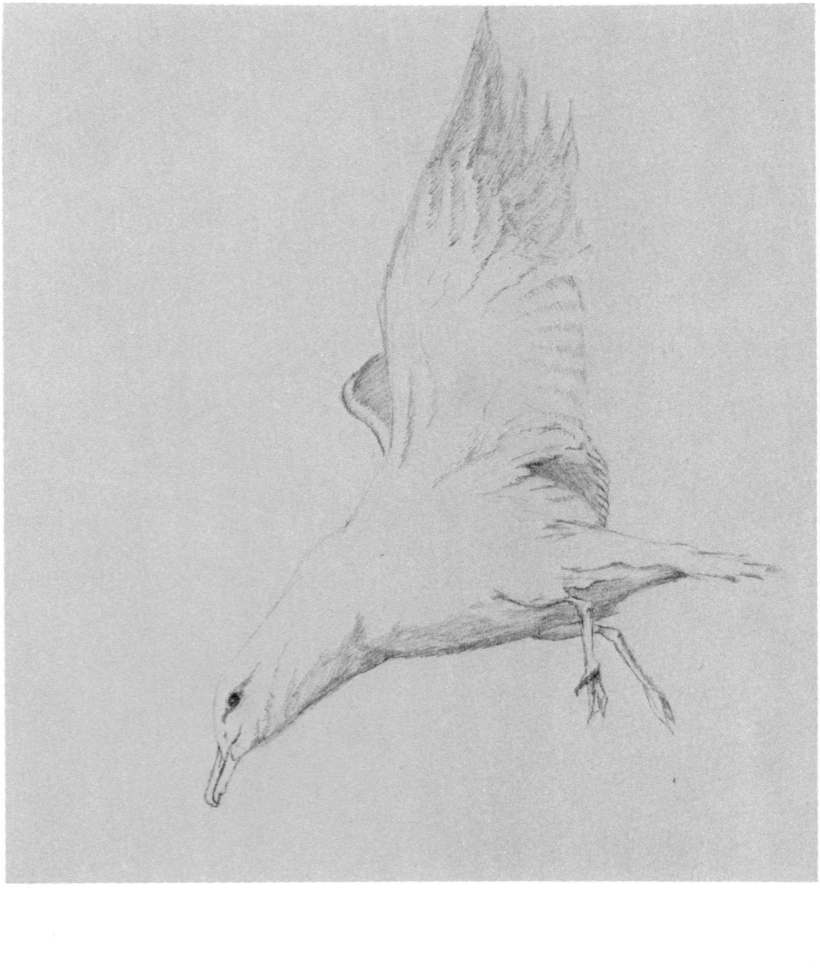

Rejoice that there is a way, that it is inevitable, and that it is so simple.

Nothing could be simpler than the way. Except straying from it.

In fear for its life, the harder will the ego struggle the closer you get.

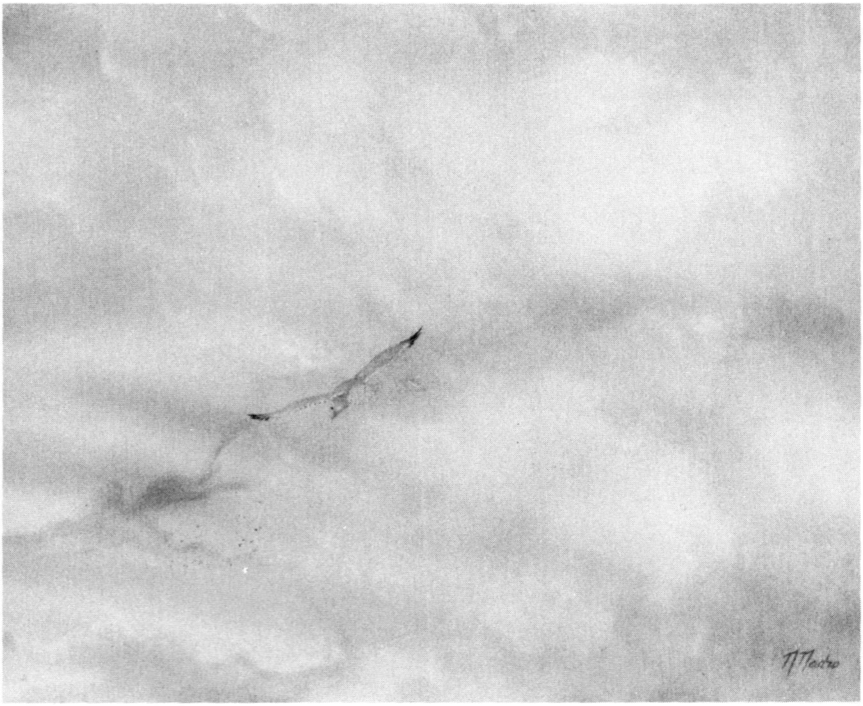

THE WAY IS TO SIMPLIFY

Consider this. You are travelling alone on a one-way trip from your hometown to a new life in a far distant land where none of your possessions will be useful or required. You have never before been out of your own country; you have not even ventured beyond your place of birth. You speak no foreign languages and have never studied the cultures and mores of other peoples. This venture you must take you recognize as inevitable and in your best interest, but the prospect of abandoning accustomed surroundings and comfortable routine for an unknown destination over unfamiliar terrain by untried means is disturbing, frightening even. How would you set out? More than likely with as little baggage as practical, so that in changing modes of transport, passing through foreign customs, proceeding afoot where necessary, you would be as unencumbered as possible, conserving your energy to accomplish the primary task: getting from here to there with as few complications, detours, delays, and setbacks as you can manage. To be sure, you would not travel naked, and you would want a reliable map, a foreign phrase book, currency conversion charts, and similar traveller's aids, but whatever did not seem likely to assist in reaching your destination, you would want to leave behind. Certainly, you would carry an item or two from home to comfort you by their association with the past, but as your new present grew increasingly fulfilling, these too you would set aside.

The way is no different. Proceeding along it demands commitment, great energy, concentration, considerable effort, and certainty of purpose. Whatever in our lives that diverts our attention from the goal, and expends energy or obscures vision, is an obstacle to forward progress, unnecessary baggage.

And yet, we are what we are, and our lives *are* complicated, filled with events, friends, desires, and habits which we enjoy, even though we can see now that they distract. We cannot, most of us, give up everything at once, and so we should not. The way will not be comfortable, but neither should it be so painful that we abandon the effort.

For now, it is enough to be aware of these things, and to ask of what we have accumulated around us how it contributes to our passage and whether it belongs with our luggage. Not with impatience or anger, but with the calm assurance that what served one purpose may not be relevant to another, and as we shift our focus from the one to the other, we can and will easily begin to let go the accouterments of the former.

The world's most frequent and experienced travellers -- diplomats, international businessmen, airline personnel -- would concur on at least this single piece of advice to the first-time tourist: travel light. Simplify.

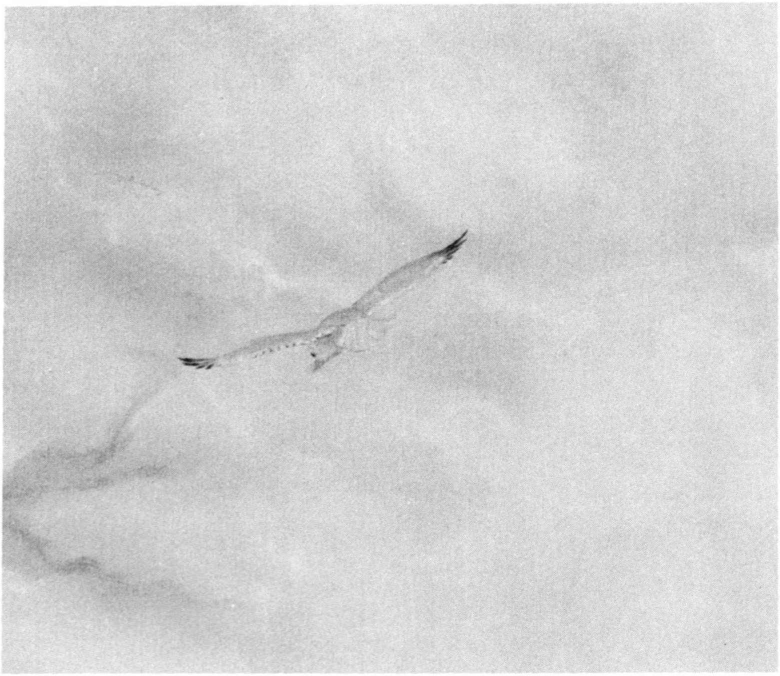

The way is to simplify.

Whatever the choice before you, choose *less* not *more*.

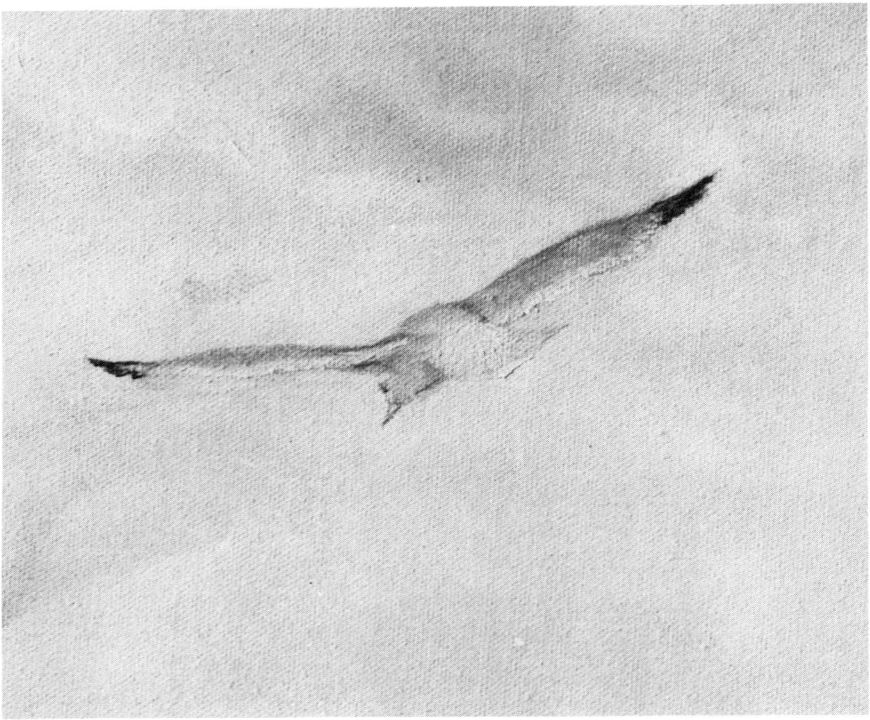

Whatever complicates is more, whatever simplifies is less.

Any answer that complicates does not solve.

The answer that simplifies is the way.

Doctrine is more. Definitions and dogma are more. Do's and Don't's are more.

Silence is less.

Seek *less*, avoid *more*.

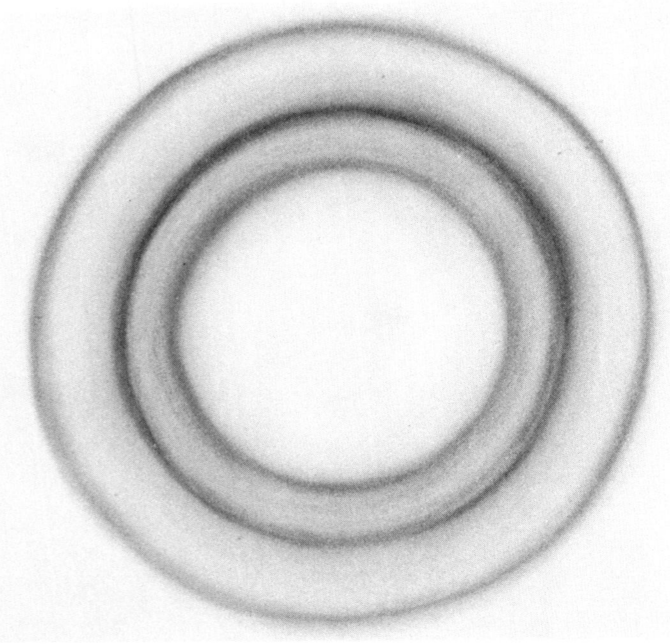

Drugs are more. Roles are more. Things are more.

The way is less.

To discard, not add on. To disengage, not encumber. To clarify, not confuse. That is the way.

The way is not a fad, cult, or belief. Neither is it a group.

Never is it *we* against *they*.

Never judge. Anyone or anything.

You simply don't have the perspective to make a case.

The way is an individual choice of the universal answer.

When to choose is our only choice.

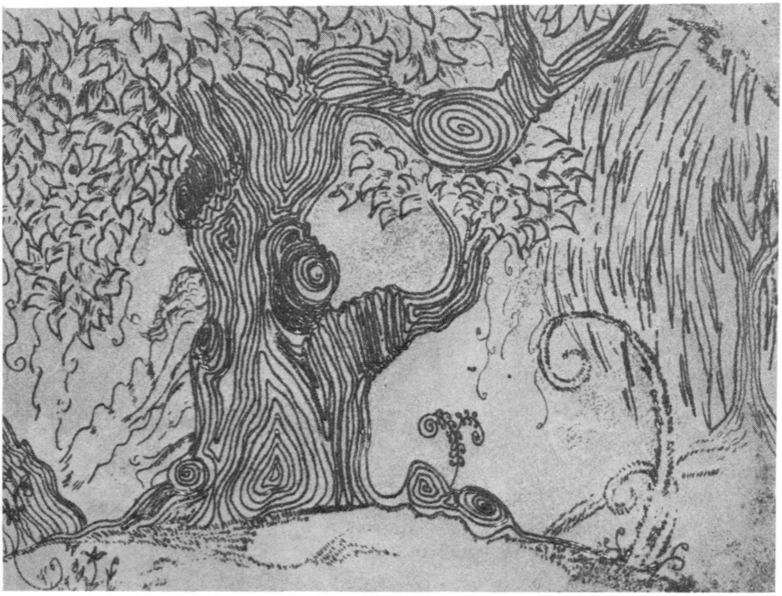

Along the way, what counts is not action, but intention. Why, not what.

If the intention is on the way, correct action will follow.

Do not resist the ego, for resistance is activity of the ego and strengthens it. Instead, simply look the other way, to the way.

Dissipation from inattention.

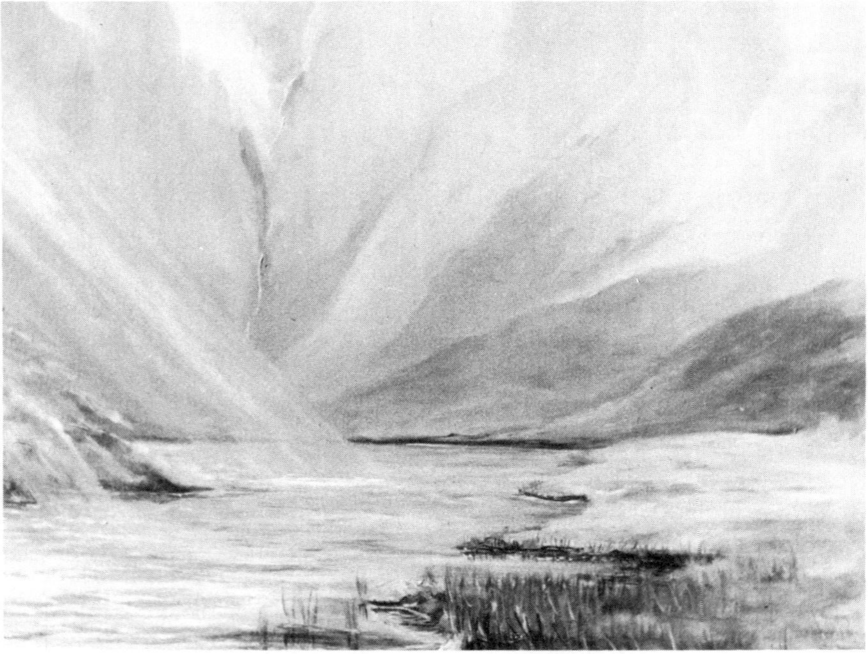

AND WHAT OF GOD?

Sooner or later along the way each of us is confronted by the question of God -- the existence and nature of a Creator. There is perhaps no issue quite so misunderstood, and it is unlikely that anything here will shed much light on the subject. Theologians of every era have struggled with this and generally speaking offered solutions which in one way or another fail to satisfy. Maybe this is an area inherently personal and ill-suited to second-hand diagnosis. Whatever the case, two things are certain: the experts have come no closer to identifying the Creator than the primitive who bows in awe before the sun (and that may be as close as we can get), and whatever else we do on the way, we will eventually wrestle the issue ourselves.

Whatever He is -- (And let us agree right off that for purposes of communication the masculine singular pronoun is as good or bad, as meaningful or meaningless, as any other; She, It, or They would be equally misleading and as inappropriate.) -- it seems clear, at least early along the way, that He is not of this world but something altogether other. To be sure, He may (or may not) manifest Himself here, but the instinctive conclusion remains that He is more than anything our eyes can see about us. Thus, we are dealing with a phenomenon at least part of which is beyond any human experience. Accordingly, any words we use to describe Him will inevitably fall short of the mark, for words are themselves a creation of this world and intended to identify or stand for its things. So, then, we might say, as some do for this reason, that God does not exist. In other words, it is impossible for our minds to conceive of Him and any conception that we might formulate is by definition inaccurate. However we define Him, He isn't.

Consider for a moment the process of definition: it is after all intended to limit its subject, to set its boundaries, to measure it. So that, if we define "tree" as roots, trunk, branches, and leaves, we have enclosed the thing, and we can confidently assert that although it grows in the soil, the tree is not itself the soil, nor is it the robin's nest that rests within it. But we cannot do that to the concept of God; no definition is adequate because a definition must (by definition!) limit and He is limitless.

Or, said another way, all of the words which we consistently and understandably use to define God, words like Infinite, All-Mighty, and Omnipresent, are themselves concepts beyond the capacity of the human mind.

While we can easily enough voice the sound represented by the word *infinite*, we cannot by that action paint a mental picture of infinity, as, for example, we can quite simply accomplish speaking the word *tree*. Infinity is beyond our mind's capacity. So is God.

If part of the difficulty lies with the limitation of language, so too at fault is our identification with the ego. The ego, you will remember, is that aspect of us which tells us that we are selves separate from other selves and other things, so that we can say "I am so-and-so, and not what's-his-name; I am a person, not a tree". And when we think of God we are similarly inclined to think of Him as a separate being. He is our Creator, we say; not us, but He who created us. He's the Father, we the children. Separate. But if God is Infinite and Omnipresent, then there can be nothing, including ourselves, that He is not, nowhere that He isn't. And that is a proposition we cannot accomodate. Not the ego, anyway. Yet, however logical and convincing this intellectual approach may seem, we are still, most of us, left with the unmistakable and continuing sense that there is a God and we want to know something about Him.

How do we proceed, trapped as we are by the dilemma in which thinking of God is senseless and not thinking of Him impossible?

Precisely as with every other obstacle along the way: we start from where we are. We recognize on the one hand that the impression we have of God at this moment is the one we have to live with for this moment, and, on the other hand, we acknowledge that that impression is inaccurate and can be accepted only subject to change, as we change. In short, we set nothing into concrete, not even, or perhaps especially, God. Remember, the way is a fluid course, and just as soon as we seem to grasp any part of it, it will change shape, preparing us to face yet another aspect of itself. Because the way has no end. And there is no point in time in which we will be able to say, "I have arrived; I understand it all".

Lest there be any fear that this approach to the Creator is somehow blasphemous, taking the name and nature of God in vain, consider this: you are doing no more than admitting the obvious, to whit, that any conception you have of God inevitably limits Him and thereby, as His creature, limits you. What you are instead trying to do, what the way itself is all about, is to remove the limits on yourself so that, free of constraints, you become free to see yourself and Him as you both (or, if it should develop this way, you One) truly are. God could want no less for you. Nor should you.

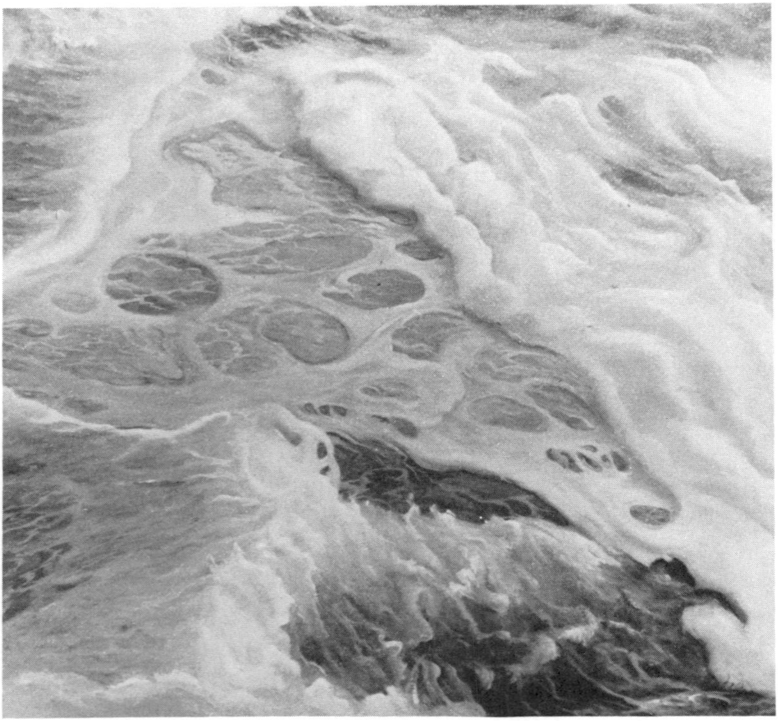

Think of God. Often.

In any way that makes sense. Or doesn't.

Male. Female. Personal. Impersonal.

Singular. Plural.

Your ego mind can't possibly conceive of God, so why try?

Because it helps to stretch, and to reach out your hand. And to be comforted.

And too, you *will* think anyway, so think thoughts which transcend thought.

Like of God.

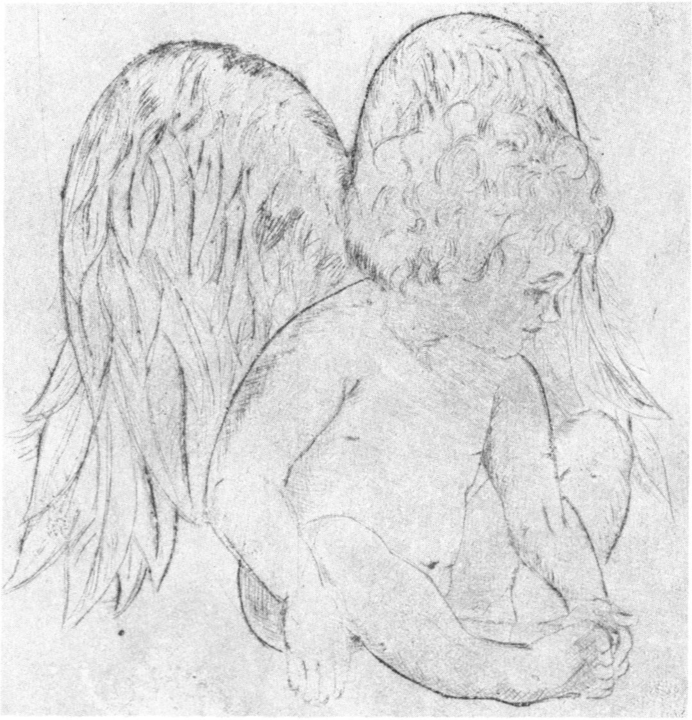

Your sense of God will change as you change. God will see to that.

Be prepared to discard the old and accomodate the new. Over and over again.

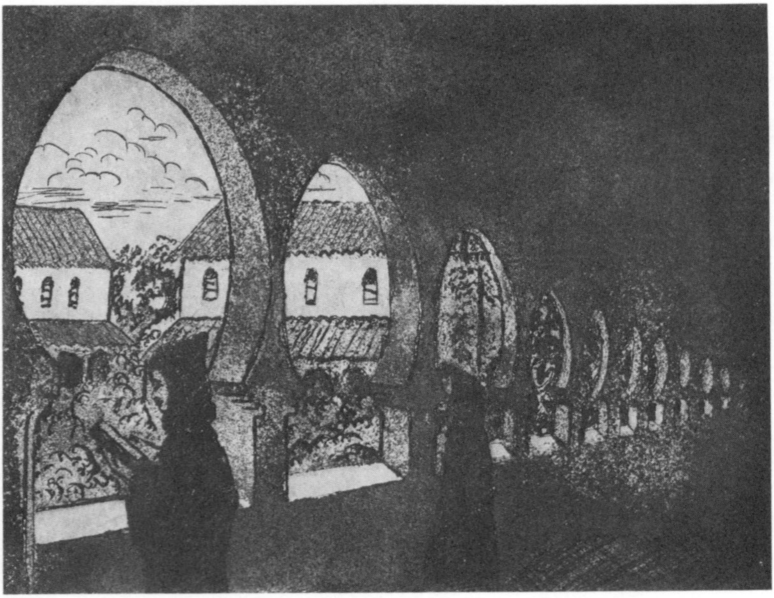

LET US PRAY

On hearing the words *Let us pray* commanded from a high pulpit, each of us dutifully kneels, bows his head, and ... what? What is it we think we are doing in prayer?

Prayer is an essential, but extremely difficult to comprehend, link between this world and all that is not of this world. Between ourselves and whatever it is we really are, what is termed here as spiritual-ness. And, perhaps, between ourselves, through this spiritual-ness, to God. It is more than just a form of communication; not a direct line to God to call His attention to our perceived problems or thank Him for their relief. None of that, of course, is necessary from His point of view, for God is, no doubt, Omniscient, and knows our needs before and better than we do. And certainly He does not depend on us for an evaluation of His performance.

Perhaps prayer is a recognition on our part that there is a Source beyond us which is not of this world but on which we are dependent for everything and from which everything comes; but also prayer is the deliberate, considered decision to put into action that recognition. Thus, prayer is acknowledging our limitations and acting accordingly.

Prayer isn't the words we speak; prayer is the way we say everything. Nor is it our deeds, but our motives behind them, and our methods. Prayer is an affirmation to God, reflected in our every breath, that we are seekers, straining to overcome the obstacles and temptations of the ego and to reach the high ground of Sight. Prayer, then, is the way.

Someone once observed that along the way we should strive to learn to want from life exactly what comes from it. Not wish for more of this or a happier that, but rather realize that our circumstances as they are represent at this moment just what we need to recognize some special aspect of the way. We say, "Praise God from whom all blessings flow"; might we restate that, "Praise God from whom all flows, and all that flows is blessing"? If we could live with that sentiment as our cornerstone, we would welcome every experience, confident that within it lies a lesson for us, guidance over an obstacle in our way.

To be sure, our minds, like their computer offspring, are linear, and can accomodate only one thought at a time. It is difficult for us to tend, for example, to our daily chores, and at the same time to have in mind the total awareness that everything we do, however menial or passing it may seem, bears directly on our progress along the way. And so we set aside times and establish exercises which will ensure that at least during certain prescribed periods we will seek that awareness. At first, these intervals may be simply a few moments each day in which we withdraw our energies from all else and focus our attention within. Eventually, we increase the frequency and length of these periods. Our methods will vary from person to person (and even from day to day) and may properly take spoken form if that is what is most comfortable at the moment. Or we may seek silence, emptying our minds of every thought, recognizing that possibly only in that way can we hope to know Reality which is not a product of our thoughts, not of this world, and can perhaps be seen only in the silence of no-thought. We label these periods as seems appropriate to us: silent moments, meditation, or simply, sitting. Or prayer.

Our goal then is to order our lives around one single all-consuming purpose and to shape our every action and thought to its fulfillment: the search for spiritual realization. Consistent, enthusiastic, and energetic attention to that goal is prayer. Non-stop communion.

So that when we hear the call "Let us pray", let us each automatically append the thought "constantly". And do.

106

Prayer is the voice of the Spirit, and it can be heard on the way.

Prayer is not an act, nor is it words. Prayer is a way of life.

Let us pray. Constantly.

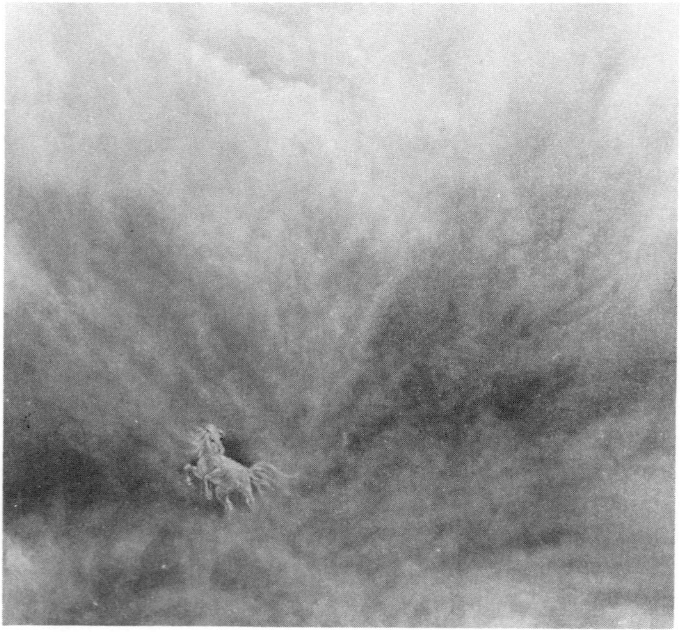

Prayer must be born within, not borrowed from without. Personal, not institutional.

Prayer is not fixed formulas or prepared texts. Prayer is the longing of the Spirit to be recognized.

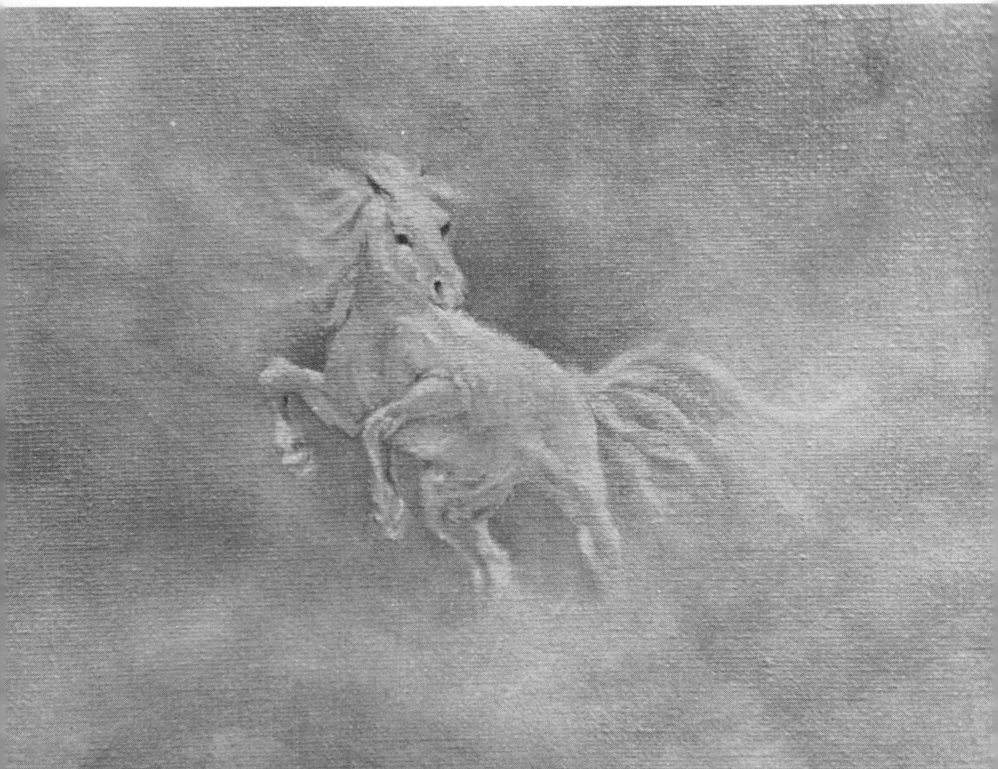

Prayer is you saying, I am not ego.

Prayer is Spirit saying, I am you.

I am.

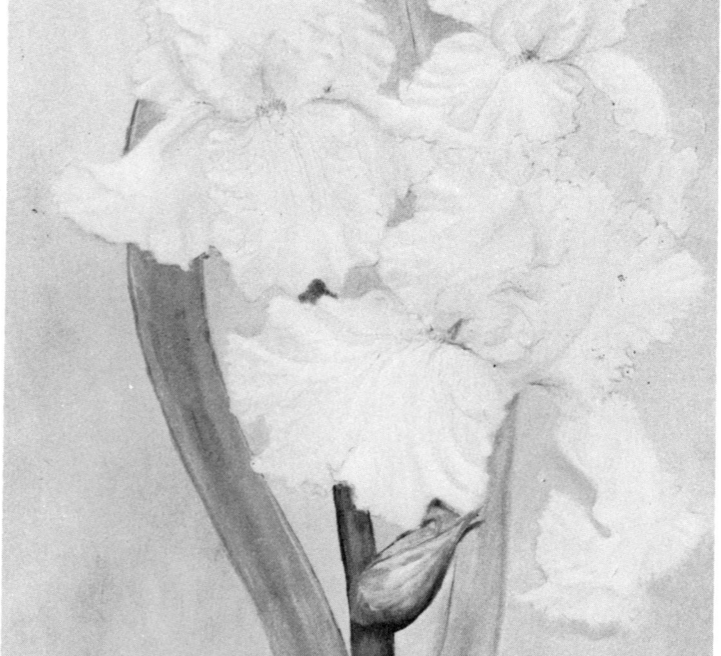

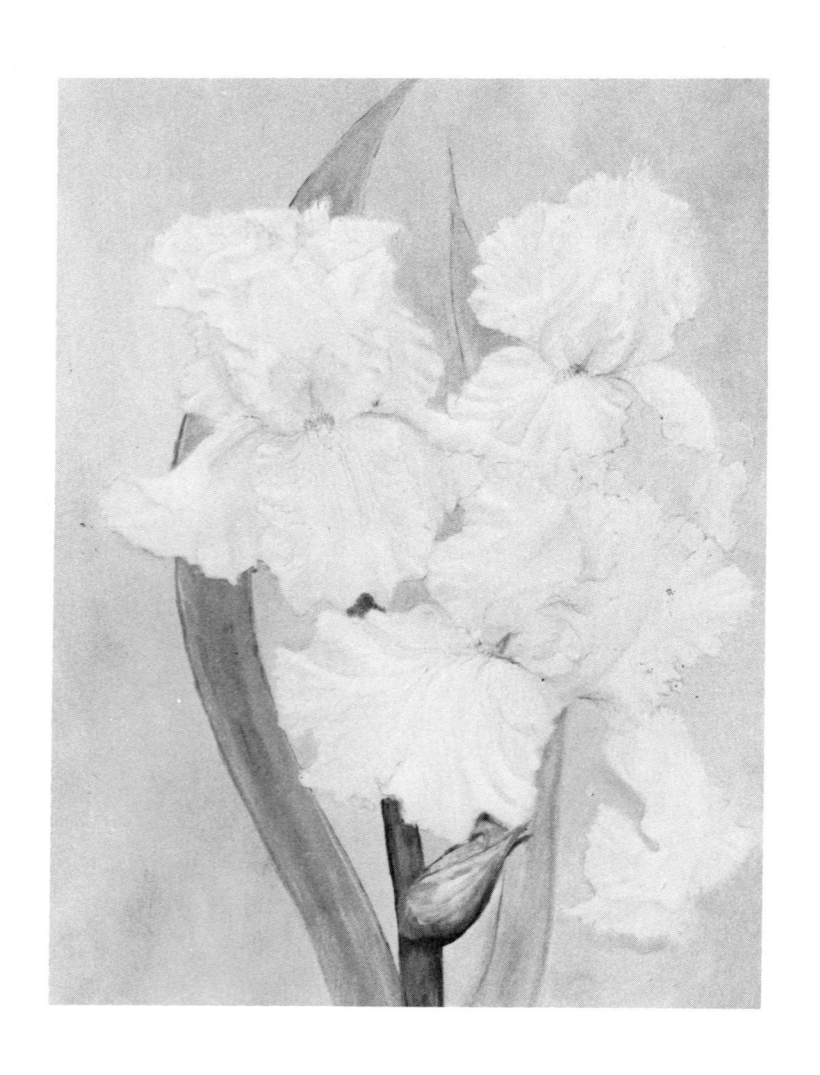

Prayer is not words. Words are a creation of the ego and describe only its things.

Prayer can be spoken, but it is not what is spoken that is prayer.

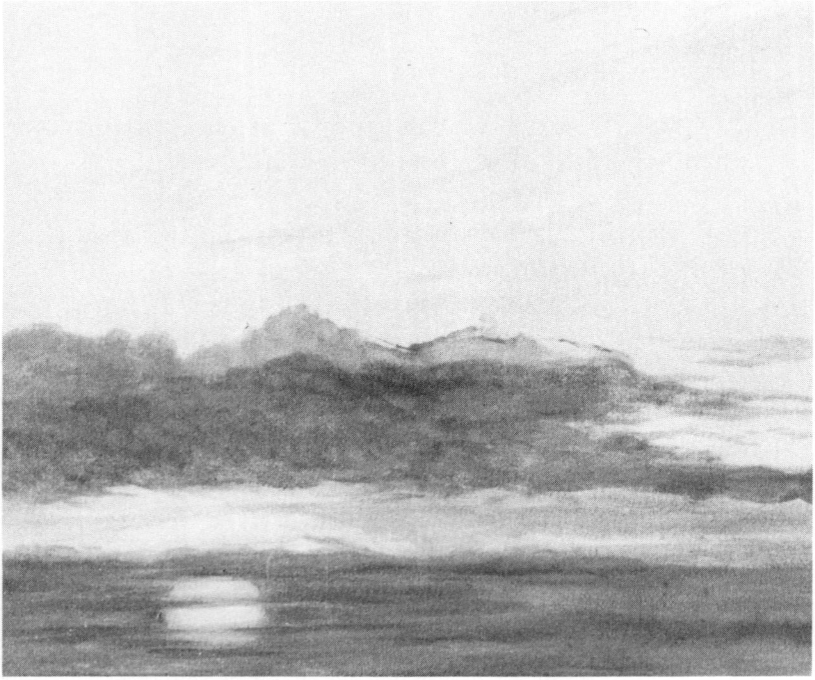

Prayer is *Let me find the way,* and seeking it.

Thy will be done, and letting it.

Prayer is surrender.

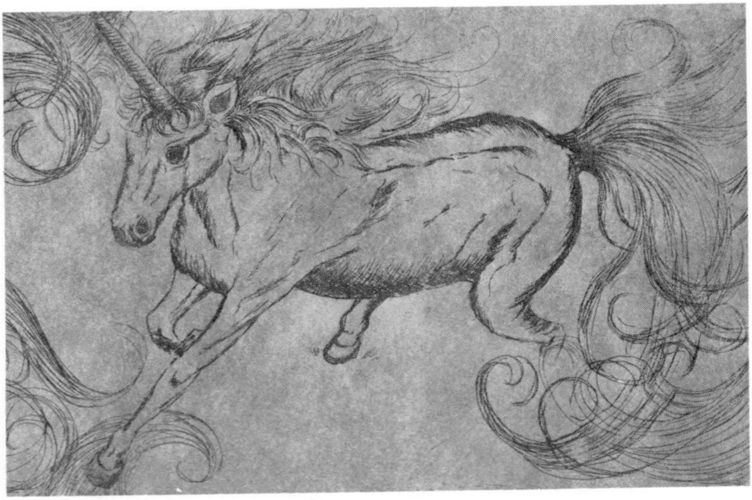

STARTING ON THE WAY

While what lies ahead can be rough going, your initial step is, as with any journey, perhaps the hardest, for it demands conscious commitment to change, to seek something other than what you have, and (so long as we see ourselves as physical) we are as subject to inertia as any matter. You have met that demand and moved, and can now proceed. The first obstacle ahead is probably already in sight, and can be overcome almost simply by recognizing it; and that is, an overwhelming sense of accomplishment, accompanied by self-congratulation, followed by complacency. Yes, you have accomplished much, but much still remains to be done. The first step *is* something, but certainly not enough.

Now, along the way, you will sense from time to time an inclination to change various aspects of your current daily life. Things that are important to you today will seem less so as you move along; others that never occurred to you as significant will loom large. As you stretch your mental faculties to encompass the unfamiliar landscape of the way, you may develop a yearning to improve your physical being, through exercises, a more sensible diet, altered habits, and the like. Your taste in books, music, films, television, and other educational and informational media may alter to reflect and enhance your new vision. Your vocabulary will change; not only will you adopt new words and phrases, but familiar ones will take on altered meaning. Other words will no longer be useful to you. In addition, as your interests become increasingly directed to your journey, you may discover yourself seeking the companionship and encouragement of others also on the way with whom to share the exploration and unfolding taking place within. All of this and more is perfectly natural, to be expected, and should be welcomed. In a very real sense, this undertaking is a rebirth, or, better, a rebirthing, and it is quite reasonable to anticipate that the new self, just now beginning to arise, will evince standards and requirements altogether different from those you now have. Let this be an evolutionary process; adapt to change when it feels right. Don't force yourself or your new self into a mold picked off a bookshelf or heard in a lecture hall. When it's time, you will know it, and then, but just then, it will fit.

    Also, be aware that as you begin to react affirmatively to the inner urge for change, those around you, accustomed to you as you have been, may be discomforted. For as you replace your old values with fresh views, those you reject are the very ones you shared until now with your current associates, and indeed may have formed the basis of the association. Your action may thus be interpreted as a rejection of themselves as persons. Threatened, their response may be defensive, even antagonistic. They may not be ready to take the step you have taken, and, as you cannot take it for them, the most you can hope to do is lead them gently to an understanding of where *you* are going. Whatever the case, don't try to push them, just as you would not want to be pushed, but neither let them inhibit your continued forward progress along the way.

Finally, no single book by a novice seeker can hope to speak with clarity and relevance to all who might read it. Indeed, it is quite likely that some will find nothing here that appeals to them, and the whole of it may seem just so much gibberish. Please let this reaction, if it be yours, not close your mind to the validity of the assertion that there is a way. As was said at the outset, the way is many. This may not be yours. But yours *is* nonetheless, and remains only to be found. All who have traversed it, in myriad languages, of diverse cultures, spanning countless centuries, agree on this one exhilarating and awesome promise: for each of us willing to seek, wherever we are and whatever our condition, there is a way.

The way is serious business, but never takes itself seriously. Or you.

So, don't.

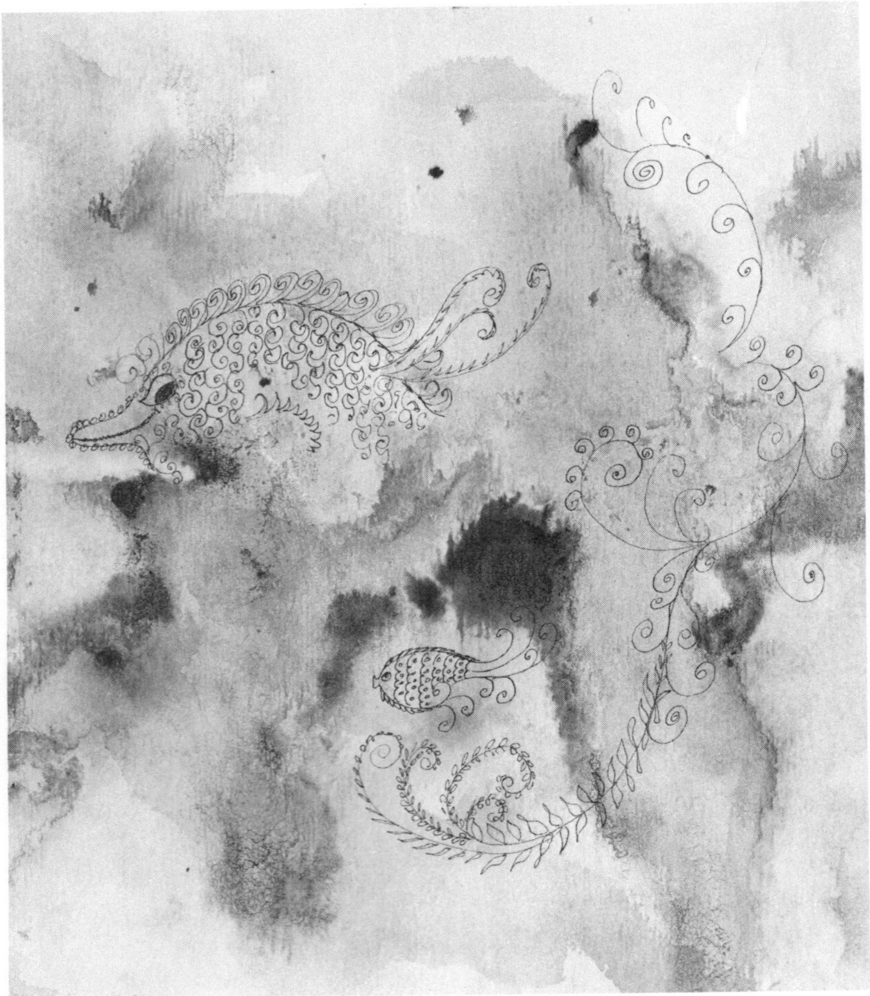

Be quick to laugh, especially at yourself. And everything else. No long faces or furrowed brows.

This is the trip of your life. Enjoy it.

Nothing is sacred, and nothing *is* sacred.

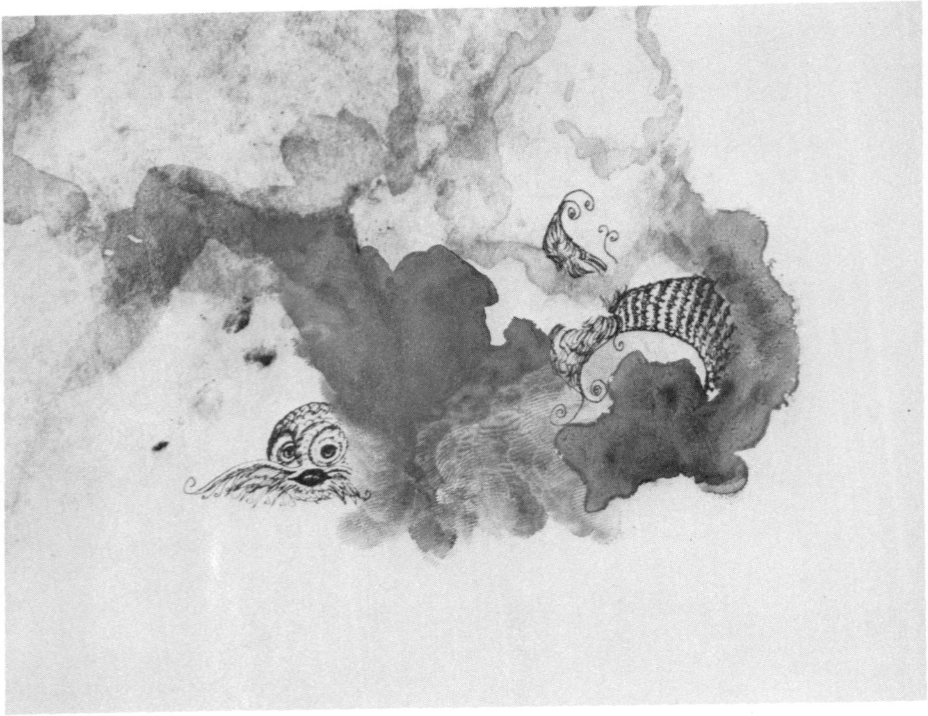

The first step is yours to make, and only you can take it. And you will.

Perhaps you already have. Perhaps you did today.

If so, you'll know it. Move along, now.

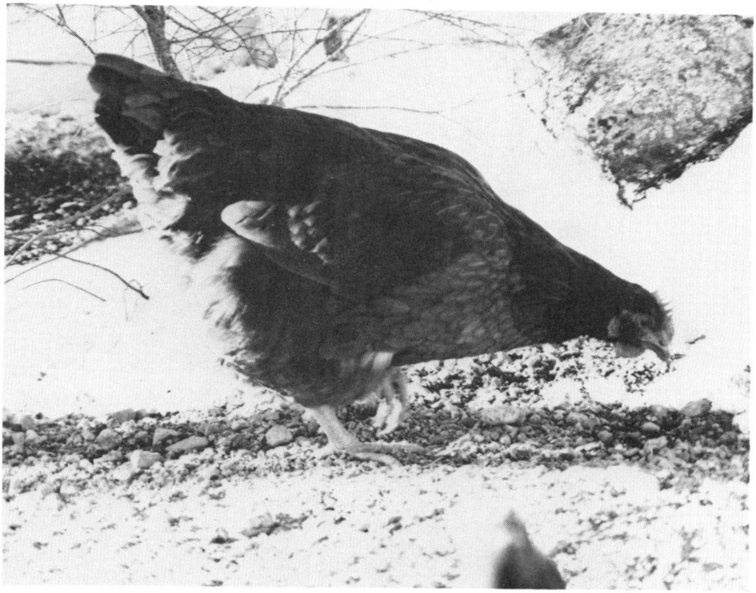